AF077386

Reflections

Artistic Poetry Vol. II

Jerrel E. Wolfe

BOOKSIDE Press

Copyright © 2022 by Jerrel E. Wolfe

ISBN: 978-1-990695-78-0 (Paperback)

978-1-990695-79-7 (E-book)

All rights reserved. No part of this publication may be reproduced, distributed, or transmitted in any form or by any means, including photocopying, recording, or other electronic or mechanical methods, without the prior written permission of the publisher, except in the case brief quotations embodied in critical reviews and other noncommercial uses permitted by copyright law.

The views expressed in this book are solely those of the author and do not necessarily reflect the views of the publisher, and the publisher hereby disclaims any responsibility for them. Some names and identifying details in this book have been changed to protect the privacy of individuals.

BookSide Press
877-741-8091
www.booksidepress.com
orders@booksidepress.com

CONTENTS

Reaching For The Stars 7
Abandoned 10
A Caring Call 15
Step Out Of The Shadow 16
Taken 18
A Solitary Tear 20
The Power of Human Touch 22
Independence Day 24
Independence Ride 27
Our Purpose 30
Today I Served 33
Dreamed Visions 37
In God We Trust 39
An Artists Dimension 41
Chicago 43
Breeching Death 46
The Postal Carrier 49
Western Beauty 51
New Beginnings 53
Katrina 55
Spared from Katrina 58
Gone 60
The Zoo Keeper 63
Origami 66
The Fishing Hole 68
Consumed by Social Pressure 71
Coming To Your Rescue 75

Healing Hands of Time	78
God's Light Show	81
Each Day	83
Outside the Box	84
The Heart Is on The Table	86
Traveling Home	89
Moving On	92
Worth the time	95
She Cared	98
Handicapped	101
Still Healing - Still Feeling	103
Let Us Win	106
Our Sanctuary	109

Reaching For The Stars

This poet is quite humbled
by words spoken here
How many lives that have been touched
how many stopped to hear

The rhyme and the meter
both have come to life
In the mastery of the pieces
I write for you tonight

It's you my faithful followers
who look into this site
Inspire me with your comments
such uplifting words you write

With you as my backbone
I venture forth from here
publish and produce this book
it's all not very clear

You say I have the talent
my words have received much praise
Labeled masterpieces by your pens
my hopes and skills you've raised

Now as I write this book
I need you all you see
You are my inspiration
my steadfast tall oak tree

I've been said to be the new blood
a storied poet of such rhyme
My name will stand with noted poets
till the end of time

Reflections

I'm trusting in your wisdom
its what's inspired me
To leap into the future
this realm of poetry

Abandoned

It was but a simple delivery
to a rest home by the bay
A place to house the elderly
and folks just thrown away

And thereupon that wrap around porch
...sitting in a chair
An aged woman with so much grace
and beautiful silver hair

I asked her if she knew a lady
named Clara Hatterly
She said, "Why yes I do young man
she sits down there... I'm one hundred three."

Each wrinkle on her smiling face
had a story to tell
And I a recent retiree
could see it all so well

Reflections

The masted ships moved serenely by
as we peered out toward the bay
She asked me to sit down a spell
and pass the time of day

Suddenly it came over me
a sense 'ner felt before
Those flowered daily deliveries
didn't mean much anymore

She smiled and said quite warmly
"I appreciate your time,
The Lord will call me home tonight
my children I can't find."

"They thought I was a burden
my needs they could not meet
They left me here ten years ago
and walked off down the street."

"Oh Johnny was a good boy
he played ball when he went to school
And Patty was a hairdresser
...worked harder than a mule."

"You know they really are good kids
just so busy don't you know
They said they'd come to see me
...that was about three Christmas ago."

...Twas then I reached out and grabbed her hand
and placed it in my palm
Told her I just saw her kids
they were at the park just singing songs

Her grandkids had new babies
all just as healthy as could be
And everyone was happy
just too busy...so they sent me

Reflections

I placed that bouquet of flowers
thereupon her lap
And told her that her family
placed all their love in that

With that came a precious smile
a grin from ear to ear
"I knew my children loved me
and that's what brought you here."

"I'm tired young man,
I have to go I need a little rest
I'll be traveling on a journey tonight,
and I need to look my best."

"Could you call the nurse before you leave
and thank you very much.
Tell my children I'll see them soon,
and I love them oh so much."

And with that said...I left her
sitting in that space
Walked out toward the setting sun
as a tear streamed down my face

I didn't even get her name
but I fell in love that day
The day I delivered flowers
to the rest home by the bay

A Caring Call

Your phone call touched my heart today
was not the words, but the way you say
"I miss you so" …lets me know
that you are here to stay

Not like the past where lies skirted the issues
or false tears on wrinkled tissues
But heartfelt love is sent my way
your soft sweet voice touches me this day

The power of the telephone
always keeps us near
It's helped to build foundation
a relationship free from fear

Self satisfied that we have spoke
and knowing you are safe
The day moves steadily forward
my heart has been embraced

Step Out Of The Shadow

Come to me from the shadows
and view me on this bed
My heart is lying open
bleeding for what my lips have not said

To entice you from your haven
and the distance that you keep
My lips are parting open
to kiss you before I sleep

I have closed my eyes and searched my soul
to find a man will not hide
One who can be close to me
and warm me deep inside

Reflections

Where's the man to fill that void
of a life that I have missed
I'll take that journey with you
and fulfill me with the gifts

Please step out of the shadows
it's the you I long to see
To impart you with gentle kisses
and stroke you endlessly

I view this vision every night
at just about half past nine
The shadowy corner of my room
where it's you I long to find

So once again I'll sleep this night
dreaming that you might come to me
Searching the shadows of my mind
for the glimpse I long to see

Taken

My baby's in your arms tonight
right where she needs to be
Rescued from a world of hate
lost morals and insanity

You know this was quite tough for me
to pass her on this way
I needed a little time to spend with her
before sending her on her way

But Lord I know you know what's best
I have total faith in you I trust
I know you have a special place
for children loved so much

If you get a chance please tell her
her mother loves her so
And tell her all about me
so her love will grow

Reflections

When we meet in heaven

and I've come home to rest

I'll thank you first for accepting her

without this earthly test

A Solitary Tear

The stain of a running tear
trickled down her face
Dripped into the water
and carried to another place

It traveled down the placid stream
all molecules still intact
This tear wasn't meant for here
and that's a simple fact

Tears are meant to dry up
with the pain of letting go
Vanish with the heat of the sun
and a heart warm afterglow

This single tear that flows right here
and travels through the night
Is searching for the answers
of who was wrong or right

Reflections

At times the search seems endless
as it travels towards the sea
And there in time it meets the brine
and melts in harmony

Were all the questions answered
as the tear flowed on its way
Or were there never any answers
to the prayers which have been laid

We as mere mortals
will have to sit and ponder this
Do all tears of sorrow
eventually lead to bliss?

The Power of Human Touch

In a world of many cultures
languages and such
There is no such power
as the human touch

It can give hope and enlighten
even bring a smile
Show the love sent from above
and cover many miles

I am a worldly traveler
...and angel...maybe so
But I find - all this pleasure
in every place I go

Reflections

I've touched the hands of Kenyans
the sick and homeless there
Traveled to the Philippines
to place hands on their hair

It's a small thing that I have to give
my smile and tender touch
But just what it does bring back
is cherished oh so much

So if you're ever needy
or need a place to pray
Or just some simple caring
to get you through the day

Know that I am with you
my touch you might not feel
You'll gain some strength from my drink
of deep love and goodwill

Independence Day

This special day comes once a year
where children marvel with delight
When fireworks fill the summer sky
and all waits for the night

It's the culmination of a day
that stands the test of time
A day we found our freedom
in a country oh so fine

Though most of us have given no thought
about this holiday
Men who fought to make this place
have died and gone away

Their names are etched on granite
their bodies rest today
They once walked this land with honor
...character led the way

Reflections

So today when you see our flag
unfurling in the sun
Remember those who came and went
...the victory they have won

Our fathers and our brothers
of centuries gone by
Planted seeds of freedom
under stars and stripes raised high

The cause was just and righteous
all countrymen could see
The future of this promised land
and their growing family tree

Even as this day grows late
and flashes fill the sky
We need to 'ner forget the fact
that men have fought and died.

Jerrel E. Wolfe

To give us such great freedom
and the independence that we know
To live in the greatest country on earth
where fireworks end the show

Independence Ride

It was early in the evening the sun had set
in a summer's pinked sky
Fireflies flashed above the flowers
it was a good night to fly

In my mind I harkened my stallion steed
from his barn this stary night
Placed the saddle on him
checked his wings for flight

His eye did shine with pleasure
for in it you could see
He knew he was about to take a trip
to the woman who saved me

No map was ever needed
my steed he always knew
Where this lady walked the earth
...he would deliver me to you

Jerrel E. Wolfe

With speed and steady pace
we crossed midwestern sky
Spotted distant fireworks
the night was speeding by

And thereupon a blanket
with eyes fixed high above
An angel viewed the bursts of light
...we were guided by her love

Although she could not see us
I took a space along her side
To watch the heavens open up
and view patriotic pride

The flashes sparkled in her eye
she had a special scent
Hair blowing in a gentle breeze
laughter that was meant

Reflections

I sat there for a while
just staring at her face
Yearning to feel her touch
caress with sweet embrace

This lady is quite special
living life from day to day
Waiting for that special moment
to give her heart away

And when that moment comes to pass
my steed and I will know
We'll view it in the western sky
and a sun setting pinked glow

Our Purpose

While God may tempt you with outside pleasures
there's no doubt he loves you so
The scale on which you measure
will decide the adorning halo

The wings sit there in heaven
rewards of life at hand...
Will they be there for eternity
with all the other specs of sand?

For how do we earn them
how do we sail this sea
Realizing all the burdens
the Lords set in front of me

While they may be heavy
He knows the weight to load
He knows just what's your breaking point
...do you choose an easy road?

Reflections

A choice made for your pleasure
is not the place to be
For each test in life you're measured
for a life in eternity

Each day we are tested
for honor faith and love
To take our place in this world
to serve the man above

When we heed our calling
to be what we shall be
To touch the lives of others
and take not selfishly

We will realize the worth
of serving in this life
To relieve all the burdens
pressures and the strife

Our accolades will be there
in a place saved for you and me
We only need to earn that place
by surviving the earthly bleed

And now today is upon us
we're here to serve again
Will we do something special this day
...or commit another sin

Today I Served

When fading sunlight meets the nighttime sky
that's the time of day I see
A waning moon shines very bright
and stars fill up an endless sea

The trees stand very still now
the leaves motionless with no breeze
There's 'ner a sound to touch the ear
no singing birds or busy bees

I take this time to reflect
on a day that has gone by
To search this empty person
to ask some questions why?

Am I here for a special reason
am I looked upon from His eye
Am I serving in his service
or just watching idle time go by

Jerrel E. Wolfe

When I look up to the heavens
and see such beauty hanging there
I seem so insignificant
...just another blank stare

I did water the flowers
fed the dogs and gave them treats
Traveled to the coffee shop
where new friends I did meet

I imparted a little wisdom
and offered up some verse
To those who seemed to listen
...it had a little worth

I spoke with my special lady
it brightened up her day
I spent time with my children
hearing what they had to say

Reflections

Prayers were issued to my friends
who lives are in disarray
There was a little cleanup
in a rather unbusy day

When you really look at it
intense it was not
But somewhere in the midst of things
I did what God has sought

It wasn't inconsequential
or trivial you see
While it could have been a little thing
it was a bigger thing for He

It was the purpose of the mission
and the fact I carried it out
That I lived my life with honor
without asking why or doubt

Tomorrow is another day
and perhaps He has a bigger plan
Until then I'll slumber...wake
and become a better man

Dreamed Visions

From masted heights I view the sea
white capped waves breaking free
Flickering light from distant land
I'm just a slave a mere deck hand

You see once I had a family
who lived on far away shore
I loved them oh so dearly
I'll never see them anymore

They've all been taken from their homes
and sailed across the sea
To toil and slave in a faraway place
With no hope just misery

Their building a mighty nation
which they say is right and just
There's great concern for all mankind
…for us there is just lust

The briny seal calls unto me
should I dive off this masted perch
Reality brings me back to life
each time this ship does lurch

Perhaps things will have changed this time
when our journey reaches port
I'll see all the smiling faces
no whips no chains no hurt

I will not be a black man
no one will notice the color of my skin
I'll set my feet on solid ground
and a new life I'll begin

It's great to dream upon this mast
where I fall asleep at night
Anticipating the coming day
when life is just and right

In God We Trust

Did you ever pause to think one day
why we say "In God We Trust"?
As you travel down life's winding road
an answer is a must

The men who built the nation
where we live free from fear
Came up with this slogan
to draw people far and near

Imagine if you lived your life
in a distant foreign land
Where oppression ruled little food
and never a helping hand

You saw a piece of currency
a special color green
A special message on it
...it couldn't help be seen

Jerrel E. Wolfe

"In God We Trust", sent a message
and an image it portrayed
Of better times a better place
...seeds of hope are laid

You see this as a calling card
to all who need our love
To offer peace and harmony
...this bill is blessed above

So when you think so selfishly
of what it might not mean to you
Think about the hope it brings
and the men who truly knew

An Artists Dimension

It doesn't take much
to slip into an artistic mode
Just stare into an empty space
and let your life unload

Travel to an emptiness
in the bottom of your heart
Open up your mind
and let your soul bring forth your art

You might write it down on paper
or place it on a canvas
Show the skill of inner will
...or orate to the masses

Whatever artistic talent
that you have found in here
Find a place to express it
for in here there is no fear

Jerrel E. Wolfe

We who can reach another level
find the next dimension
Realize life's real beauty
in a gift of perfect vision

Chicago

The car sped around the corner
the gun went rat-a-tat
I pictured myself on a Chicago Street
about seventy-five years back

I stood there with my sweetheart
with her fine haberdashery
Huddled up against the wall
in hopes gangster bullets were not meant for me

The windows in that corner shop
were shattered on the ground
And stepping from the lacquered Packard
two well dressed thugs did abound

They made their way past the rubble
and entered through the screen
Returning with a stately man
whom I had never seen

Jerrel E. Wolfe

They placed him in the waiting car
and then just sped away
Leaving frightened pedestrians
to watch in sheer dismay

A common sight on city streets
in an era when gangsters ruled
Storekeepers learned to keep mouths shut
for lessons of oppressive violence had been schooled

We continued down the darkened street
and near a far streetlight
We heard the sound of Duke's big band
...Care to Charleston tonight?

Past the guarded entrance
into the smoke filled hall
The flappers and the dappers
were having quite a ball

Reflections

There was alcohol a plenty
and damsels ruled the night
Gentlemen with slicken hair
were visioned left and right

A ragtime tune scorched the air
as the patrons laughed with glee
Another round of bootleg...
rot gut whiskey for you and me

This time...the roaring twenties
is Americana of the past...
I WAKE...with etched memory
an era that couldn't last

Breeching Death

There she blows yelled the bows man
as he stood upon his perch
Peering out into the ocean
to view the reason for this search

Magnificent and elusive
this whale of the raging sea
Now became the prey of man
and a hunt that tortured me

I had 'ner set foot on a vessel
and ventured from a port
But sometimes as a journalist
we must take adventures of this sort

I felt a fear come over me
as the men prepared the gun
The crew had filled the chase ship
...the mission had begun

Reflections

This blue whale breached the surface
the gun discharged its spear
Past the spewing brine
the harpoon hit its mark so dear

The crew of the chase boat
held on for the ride of their life
Ultimately for the prey they sought
this whale would undergo the knife

Now as I sit here
dim light of day cast on horizon
The workers fill the casks of oil
numbered by the dozen

Each piece of meat is tucked away
upon this merciless ship
And I just sit and wonder
what's the point in all of it

...This story I brought home with me
this whale now lights our town
Each evening when the lamps are lit
I hear echoes of his dreaded dying sound

The Postal Carrier

Winter's air comes quickly
as autumns leaves fall from the trees
The crisp bite of the morning
says pull out the longer sleeves

Those days of tanning sunshine
are dwindling very fast
The warmth of a shallow sun
cast longer shadows and makes me ask…

What purpose do the seasons have
and why do they come this way
Autumn's harvest of covered fields
yields to snow covered piles of hay

With the frozen nature becomes quite still
the birds have left the sky
No morning sounds as I make my rounds
for this delivery guy

Jerrel E. Wolfe

A crunch is heard beneath my feet
as I tread through hardpack snow
I yearn to see the spring again
my frosted cheeks now glow

A cup of coffee warms my heart
I'll seek to stay inside
Till the morning calls once again
and I cast my warmth aside

Western Beauty

I see beauty in a sunrise
as the light breaks through the trees
I see beauty in the clouds above
as they move with gentle breeze

There's beauty in those mountain peaks
the tips of snowy white
Beauty where the eagles soar
their wings spread out in flight

It's there upon the prairie
wild mustangs come and go
There's beauty in the butted flats
majestic sentinels standing in a row

There's beauty each and every day
in the high country that I see
Rock formations rivers
and all that's there for me

Jerrel E. Wolfe

I couldn't live the city life
the hassle every day
I need the open spaces...
God's country you might say

So for you I pose this question
as you slave your life away
Will you ever seek a quest
to see life in a different way

If this piece has moved you
and the beauty's etched your mind
Take a trip to the wild wild west
and see what you might find

New Beginnings

The conductor yelled "All Aboard"
the train steamed clouds of white
Passengers grabbed a final kiss
as they boarded this autumn night

The crispness of the evening air
mixed with the smell of cast iron steel
Brought an air of excitement
for all passengers to feel

East coast to the West coast
in just seven days I'm told
Riding on this steel clad horse
where a new life will unfold

St Louis, Virginia City and then
the city by the bay
A chance to start a new life
as I sit back and pray

Jerrel E. Wolfe

In my past I leave behind me
the Big Apple and all its sights
The trials and tribulations
of the violence and street fights

My family has all passed away
and I must seek my fate
Ride the rails and seek the trails
to the home I hope to make

There's a lady in my future
and a nest for us to share
I'll search my soul to find the path
that will take me there

There's always new beginnings
one just has to take the step
Find the courage to move forward
and not look back with regret

Katrina

They called the storm Katrina
Gulf shores lie in its path
The fury of King Neptune's Sea
destined destruction from its rath

The media pronounced its coming
category five they'd come to know
But not during this lifetime
had they envisioned such a show

Evacuation and strict curfews
were the order of the day
Not much else could be done
except to board up coastal cities
Then sit back and pray this day

Decades had gone by
no one had seen a storm like this
No seniors to huddle families
with stories to reminisce

Jerrel E. Wolfe

She slammed ashore that August morn
turned east of the Big Easy
Crushing wooded houses
and covering the earth with sea

It took out Biloxi
Gulf Shores and Mobile Bay
Swept away the lives
of many who chose to pray

Thirty-foot walls of water
came crashing on these shores
Leaving just the rubble
for mortal men to do the chores

There's not a true American
who lives upon this land
That hasn't felt this in his heart
and wants to lend a hand

Reflections

We feel this as a nation
and together we unite
If with nothing more than empathy
we join our brothers in this fight

Yes Katrina you've crashed our shoreline
with the power you possess
Scorched our southern beaches
and brought unhappiness

But you as mother nature
have not beat us in this test
It's just a minor setback
in the Freedom we've been blessed

Spared from Katrina

Across from the Brewery
sits the local park
I had a chance to walk by there
just a little before dark

This autumn eve where leaves did fall
from the mighty oak tree's arm
Gave me a chance to view the dance
of the gray squirrel's subtle charm

There was music in the background
scent of coffee in the air
I knew that I was being blessed
for having traveled there

Erected on the centered pulpit
stood a bronze man known to all
The president of the confederacy
a nation born to fall

Reflections

Past that mounted soldier
just outside the gate
A tower reaching up to heaven
pointing toward our final fate

I see this park as God's land
as He views it every day
From the cross atop the peak
where He looks for us to pray

So should you ever have the chance
to visit New Orleans of today
Remember God spared this park
so we could sit and pray

Gone

The factory stands abandoned
there upon the hill
The parking lot is empty
no production all is still

The era of the steel mills
has come and gone this day
Leaving heaps of rubble
along this interstate highway

No darkened plumes pouring
from the towering smoke stacks
No engines or rail cars
moving down rusted railroad tracks

Today's generation
hasn't even come to know
The lifetime that surpassed them
and the lives affected so

Reflections

Not only did this industry
produce the foundation of this land
It fueled the fires of entrepreneurs
with a vibrant economy to be fanned

Happy weddings, anniversaries
vacations with children dear
Jobs for nearly everyone
no street violence to fear

Life was such a simpler time
when gas was thirty cents
The ease of which to purchase food
and inexpensive rents

The women were more wholesome
the men still wore top hats
Family values were instilled in kids
and morals were intact

Oh today we deal with changes
and that's real life for you and me
But once... for an older generation
harmony was reality

The Zoo Keeper

Each day of life's a blessing
my work's become part of me
Tending to God's creatures
and loving them you see

I can hardly wait to punch the clock
and walk upon their land
The excitement is continually building
as they kiss my outstretched hand

The monkeys scream with pleasure
as they swing around their cage
The bears stand up and raise their paws
as if actors on a stage

The otters take their morning dip
and wave their flippers up to me
The seals bark out a morning chant
as I look into their sea

Jerrel E. Wolfe

A giraffe reaches down I scratch his chin
and pat him on the nose
"Feel the love my tall friend
from your head down to your toes."

The lions and the tigers
purr with my loving touch
The world thinks they're so viscous
"I think not very much."

The llamas congregate around the fence
to greet me every day
The birds walk in my footsteps
in hopes something might fall their way

There's so much joy and pleasure
in the job that I hold here
I feel kind of like a Noah
time passes year to year

Reflections

Not too much has changed here
in my thirty years in this place
God's creatures appreciate the care I give
and await my smiling face

You too will be accepted
when you enter through the gate
Bring the children have a picnic
enjoy the zoo…please don't wait

Origami

Take a piece of paper
fold the edges tweak a knot
Flip it over start again
and see just what you've got

They call this art Origami
for what reason I don't know
It's just a folded paper
a bird a box a bow

From just a simple piece of parchment
an art form you will find
Just use your imagination
it doesn't matter if you're blind

There's something very soothing
to fold and give away
The treasures that you make up
when your heart folds gifts this way

Reflections

At Christmas there are angels
with wings arched from their back
Easter bunnies and springtime flowers
and various knicks and knacks

You'll charm the eldest senior
and place smiles upon young faces
This art of Origami
will take you many places

So the next time you undertake a challenge
to see what you can do
Fold a simple piece of paper
it's Origami when your through

The Fishing Hole

I see my grandson's freckles
as he sits beneath the tree
Fishing pole in hand
staring intently as can be

I've fished this hole since '31
and it's been real good to me
Fed my struggling family
with the fish the Lord provided me

For years now it's just been a pleasure
to come down to this old stream
Catch a few release a few
and just sit back and dream

Not too much has changed here
when I view it from where I stand
Sure the highways and the cities
have grown all across the land

Reflections

But you see it's still quite peaceful here
this is where I use to play
Now in my twilight years
I'll pass it off today

Grandson why don't you sit down here
next to your old granddad
I want to share a special gift
handed down from my granddad

From today on this is your spot
a place to dip your pole
Respect this sanctuary
it's now your fishing hole

The Lord's seen fit to give me space
to ponder life's great tasks
And now that you enter manhood
this is all I'm gonna ask

Jerrel E. Wolfe

Each time you fish this fishing hole
check the man you have become
Make the needed changes
so your world won't be overrun

Live your life with honor
good deeds and be of cheer
Don't forget to check yourself
each and every year

If in time a little left of here
you hear a big old splash
Pay no mind just smile and know
It's me... pulling out a big ole bass

Consumed by Social Pressure

My son was just an average boy
about the age of ten
I saw in him a caring soul
and lots of love within

He was oh so precious
and I loved him so each day
I often thanked the lord above
for sending him this way

He has always been a special boy
and no doubt will always be...
Despite the hurt and all my pain
...and recent agony

For you see he was a victim
of a social blight
Influenced by the kind of man
with money in his sight

It was but a token gift
to chase the blues away
A substance he found he needed
each and every day

Life for my boy wonder
began to fall apart
He lacked appreciation
and feelings from the heart

And now it was a twenty
and heroin you see
His sweetness of adulthood
was drowning in the sea

Reflections

I threw him many jackets
and lifeboats for to enter
But to the power of the twenty
he ultimately surrendered

My life is filled with chaos
and I often wonder why
God would do this terrible thing
to my special little guy

Or time I've come to look upon it
and see it differently
I know now…it's but just time
…till he comes back to me

He will get all that is needed
and come to appreciate the love
And no doubt gets to know
that noble man above

Yes son I still love you
...you know I always will
I know I'll find that little guy
...it's just some time until

Coming To Your Rescue

I slumbered in a chair one night
with dreams of my winged steed of white
And how blessed that I could be
to travel through the world with he

This special gift I was given
today I know not why
He came my way one special day
to fly the late night sky

To correct all the sorrows
to sooth your agony
To carry this mortal angel
sharing heart and soul for thee

We've healed the hearts at Columbine
and dressed the World Trade Center's mess
Saved several broken souls
and laid heroes' ghosts to rest

We travel on any given night
across the starlit sky
With wings spread wide and a flashing glide
to be there by one's side...

You will never ever see us
for God's chosen this — not to see
We are just to be there
delivering a gift from He

So when your heart is heavy
and your burdens out of sight
Look to the heavens up above
and seek your guiding light

Reflections

This stallion steed of wonder
his whiteness in the night
Carries hope aboard with shining sword
and your angelic valiant knight

Healing Hands of Time

The Grandfather clock stands etched in time
in the silence of the room
Motionless hands frozen
once happy home is filled with gloom

The children sit in wonderment
and I in deep repose
Staring into the silence
not knowing where life goes

The candle here does not burn as bright
as when once two candles glowed
There's heartaches and questions
in this place that's our abode

Reflections

You see there is no mother
I the father holds the reins
Left with a task to carry on
despite life's agonizing pains

She said she loved her children
her husband but not her life
The burden was too heavy
filled with too much stress and painful strife

If cheating was the answer
there's one happy soul today
While three others just ask - why
and live through another day

Now as life continues
I see a need for this
To pull the chains of father time
and hear the chimes of bliss

With slow melodic motion
the hands begin to move
Leaving stagnation in the past
and hearts with heavy grooves

With each minute that now passes
there's healing in the heart
We begin to pick up the pieces
of a love that fell apart

The chimes of this stately clock
now fall heavy on the ear
As time goes by their beauties bliss we'll find
as we move from year to year

God's Light Show

Meteors showered the midnight sky
as crescent moon kissed the night
The cool spring breeze caressed my neck
as I looked up in delight

The beauty of this place we live
and the happenings that do occur
Place me in awe at times
emotions continually stir

Aircraft at 30,000 feet
do they know the beauty just above
Do the windows hold the glory
of nightly skies of which I love

The Dipper and Orion
the north star shining bright
Just a real small part
of this majestic night

Jerrel E. Wolfe

From where or why or how
these occurrences come to be
Will never truly be known
not by you or me

For God has chosen this light show
on this summer's night
And filled it with the richness
of his empowering light

Does he do this for excitement
or for us to look above
To stop us from our daily chores
to seek a heavens love

For each happening has a reason
The Lord has made it so...
What message will I read into this tonight
before to bed I go

Each Day

In the shadows of a darkened room
I hear your whispers
In the cool breeze of an autumn day
I feel your touch

In the garden of this mansion
I grasp your flowered scent
In the heat of the sunlight
I sense your warmth upon my neck

In each drink that passes o'er my lips
I taste your tender kiss
And each moment that I live this life
your presence I do miss

Outside the Box

Before being wed, I ne'r took to bed
the man I would eventually marry
The thoughts of this within God's sight
was simply just too scary

To wait we did
and so we found a special situation
Where just he and I beneath God's eye
cherished a special occasion

The love was deep and ours to keep
it was more that I could ask for
For in this love sent from above
we could open any door

The years went by sharing times that fly
with burdens fights & sorrows
Then the love we had in times good and bad
filled the yesterdays and tomorrows

Reflections

But then one day I sat in dismay

my heart just crushed and broken

To my husband and my soulmate

I was just another token

To cope with all my hopes and dreams

dashed upon the rocks

I came to the realization

...he sought love outside the box

The Heart Is on The Table

Lying on the table
with the surgeon in my heart
Repairing all the damage
that life has torn apart

She has me at her mercy
she controls the ebb and flow
Of the life I've yet to live
and the roads that I must hoe

Her fingers must be gentle
it's the dexterity there in she
Not to bruise the tissue
or further injure me

Reflections

When closure has been made
and the body has been healed
I'll take the blows upon that chest
her repairs won't come unsealed

I'll have a life back in control
where hope and loves a must
I'll only open up my heart
to the one that I can trust

But right now I still lay on the table
the surgeon at my side
To fix me well save me from hell
with stiches that's been tied

Great healers there are many
and surgeons walk this earth
Saving man from danger
and children at their birth

They have only one intention
and that's to do their job just right
When they go to bed and night
they pray for more insight

It's not just with the hands and precision
they work their trade
but the bedside manner
for complete recovery must be made

Traveling Home

Ice cold and weak and trembling
I could see no hope for me
I threw up a final prayer to God
and sank beneath the sea

I pictured myself sinking
air bubbles drifting upward past my face
A serenity surrounded me
the Atlantic I did embrace

The glide was slowly downward
inside there was no panic
And there just an arm's reach from me
a sinking ship... Titanic

It slid past me into the depths of night
the depths of a great unknown
Angled towards its final resting place
a place to be its home

In the distance through the brine
I saw a great white light
Consuming earthly creatures
in a night filled with utter fright

Pressure built inside me
as if a force was to be set free
Then I felt the hand of God
rest itself on me

This vacuum of overwhelming white
consumed my being's space
Hearing faintly in the distance
angelic Amazing Grace

I heard Dad's unique laughter
mother's voice... and now a vision
Uncles aunts and family passed
received me from my mission

Reflections

This was a true homecoming
one I 'ner thought I should see
The night of the great Titanic
slipped beneath the ice cold sea

Moving On

Life is very fleeting
though it doesn't really seem so
Until you take a look back
at how fast the children grow

It seemed the early years
would never come to pass
With doctor visits nighttime crying
hoping to get a grasp

But now with quick reflection
those days did fly by so
A little girl has become a lady
and off to college she will go

Her aspirations set high
morals all intact
A woman with her own mind
goals and all of that

Reflections

The next ten years will come and go
faster than the rest
My daughter will begin a journey
the future she will test

A lady possessing all the tools
to travel down the road
Finding love and marriage
a nest and her abode

Just as she was a young child
adolescent and a teen
Life is ever changing
the path not clearly seen

A father who holds her dearly
told stories along the way
Continues to look forward
to her shining day

Jerrel E. Wolfe

There will be much joy and laughter
laced with heartache and sorrow
An emotion laden rollercoaster
that we all have come to know

It all makes life worth living
the sunshine and the rain
The forces working for and against us
that keep us in the game

Pride touch and nurturing
has brought forth all of this
Today I send her down the road of life
with love and a parting kiss

There will often be times I reflect on this
her final parting day
And think of all the joy in life
brought forth from the girl called Shea

Worth the time

She came to spend some time with them
she came to spend the day
To give them love and support
as they struggle along the way

She has a heart of gold you see
and a love transcending the seas
She can see deep into their hearts
and hear their silent pleas

They call her Grum for the fun
...that a grandmother can be
Always there with words of care
and insight for to see

Laughter comes back to the kids
and hearts begin to show
The love inside and fears they hide
...they don't want the world to know

Jerrel E. Wolfe

This weekend that you that you chose for them
was oh so very special
For you know they've done life's chores for you...
and with pride they seek approval

Life has delt some real harsh blows
and children become weary
The who's what's when's and why's
...are really very scary

A couple of teenagers
searching for answers every day
Need a loving grandmother
to help release the words they pray

For in her they see mother
whose no longer in their life
The sentinel of a loving mom
whose cut them with the knife

Reflections

The knife of rejection
lost love the children feel
Grandmother knows the things they speak
are very far from real

She knows her sibling deep inside
and shares her love this day
Knowing that her daughter
would want it to be this way

When this nightmare's ended
and daughters on solid ground
Grum will pass her torch of love
and grandchildren back around

But today the story still plays out
...a journey's being taken
A journey to save the souls
of children whose been forsaken

She Cared

She said she didn't like it
the piano just no way
Forced to take those lessons
the parents' child obeyed

For years there was reluctance
quite stubborn that she was
Somehow someway we knew this child
would benefit from us

When parents look to the future
and provide a loving light
Children can't appreciate
their wisdom and foresight

The drudgery of lessons
when childhood is for play
To sit and practice endlessly
on sunny summer days

Reflections

We question if it was worth it
to spend the money so
To give the child a little gift
to carry through the life she'll come to know

Tonight it was all worth it
as I sat upon that chair
To hear her stroke the keyboard
and music fill the air

You see it has been years
since she sat upon that bench
Practiced simple tunes
while threatened by a fist clenched

I had all but given up
thinking this art she would never know
Until tonight with great delight
she filled my heart with glow

Jerrel E. Wolfe

She remembered all the structure

the notes clefs and keys

That gorgeous sound was heaven bound

and for me certain to please

That child became a lady

and took a gift you see

Paid it back with dividends

in the songs she played for me

Handicapped

Today I realize I'm handicapped
my futures plain to see
I will travel throughout this life
with a piece missing from me

No it's not an arm or leg
or a physical infirmity
I've lost the one I gave my love
for all eternity

It cannot be recovered
no surgery can mend
A love that was dishonored
by a wife and bonded friend

It's a handicap a burden
to carry down the road
A challenge meant to overcome
it's just part of the load

So life moves on I'll do my best
working through the added stress
Accepting all the blessings given...
to seek the Lord's planned success

Still Healing – Still Feeling

Today I sit in a place
I dare not want to be
Thinking of the one I love
so far away from me

The caring soul that saved me
from a catastrophic mess
Now finds her love enslaved to me
challenged by this test

There is no other woman
whom I love and hold so dear
But emotions seem to wain a bit
...I hurt and still have fear

I'm told it really takes a while
to get over a love now passed
Even when it seems like this
is just inches from my grasp

This wretched soul keeps climbing
the walls to be set free
But somehow never gets there
past love is holding me

With rationale and reason
I know I must move on
To find my destined future
and sing a different song

My new love oh so wonderful
is stagnant in the mist
Waiting for my heart to release
the anger of past bliss

Reflections

To look into the future
is very hard for me
And so this person in my past
is purged with poetry

The Lord My God has given me
this talent to posses
Soon my heart and soul shall sail
to a newfound happiness

I can't control the currents
or help the wind to blow
I must be patient in the fact
the futures His you know

Let Us Win

Just a hit just one more run
that is all we really need
Please dear God let us win this game
my ego needs to feed

I've done my best and worked so hard
Please don't give up on this team
My parents are intently watching ...
it's the only game they've seen

(later)

The last time I spoke to you
I ask you for your help

You ignored my plea to rescue me
and save my team today
You left me down without a sound
I no longer wish to play

Reflections

(In a dream)

Hello dear son who ask of me
such a small request
I heard your call to control that ball
and grant your happiness

Don't think that I ignored you
there was a lesson learned today
I looked down upon you
and decided things this way

I could make one team happy
I could make one team sad
There were 18 prayers said to me
some from coaches some from dads

I held in admiration
the trust you placed in me
I honor your commitment
and the fact that you're Godly

Jerrel E. Wolfe

Your old enough to understand
the problem dealt to me this day
And why I had to sit back
and enjoy the way you play

You really didn't lose this game
you won it from the start
We all cheered in heaven
when you opened up your heart

Our Sanctuary

There's a place that all great poets go
to spill their thoughts and clear their heads
A place that's distant from today
a new dimension it's been said

We travel to this hollow space
and commune within our mind
Flowing verse to paper
that generations are sure to find

A little bit of feeling
love pain and memories
It's what we find within us
we share in hopes to please

If we are successful
to have you read it twice
Think about the meaning
and heed its sound advice

Jerrel E. Wolfe

We know as poets we have become
what life was meant to be
A shining star within your sky
in the universe of poetry

www.ingramcontent.com/pod-product-compliance
Ingram Content Group UK Ltd.
Pitfield, Milton Keynes, MK11 3LW, UK
UKHW041943230426
12048UKWH00008B/95